MW00905136

Contents

Before you Begin:

1. In addition to everything you'll learn in this book, practice songs as well! Everything you learn should be applied within songs.
2. You'll find it helpful to invest in a metronome, a good seat, and a few pairs of sticks!
3. Drumming can be overwhelming when you're first starting; there are a lot of things to think about and many pieces to keep track of. Try to focus on one thing at a time and take it slowly.
4. If you're learning a song or rhythm, don't try to play it quickly at first, even if you think you can. Slowing things down can be harder than playing fast, not only will you be challenged, you'll also be able to focus on your technique.
5. Listen to all styles of music, be it rock, blues, jazz, or metal, and look for new (and old) bands as well. Exposing yourself to all different kinds of rhythms is a great way to increase your creativity and your musical vocabulary.
6. Have fun, it doesn't matter what you're doing, but you might as well enjoy doing it! We all start somewhere; just know that, with practice, you'll get to where you want to be.

If you need drum tablature, blank music, or other practice material, you can find it at LutzAcademy.com (along with free lessons!). If you have any music-related questions, our online community will be happy to help! It's free to join and is filled with likeminded musicians of all levels and backgrounds.

Beginner Basics

Drums & Cymbals
Drum kits come in many different sizes and styles. There are hundreds of cymbals to choose from and thousands of drum combinations. Most people will start with a five piece kit or smaller. For the majority of book 1, you'll only need three pieces of your kit. As you get more experienced, you can add and change your drums and cymbals to fit your needs. Below, we've explained the most important parts of your set.

Snare Drum

This is the drum that will sit at the center of your kit, directly in front of you in between your legs. On the bottom of the snare drum, you'll find snares which can be engaged and disengaged via a lever on the side. Typically, you'll want to keep them engaged (raised and touching the bottom head of the drum) so that you can hear them ring when you hit the top of the snare.

Bass Drum
The bass drum can be found on its side, on the floor. This drum is played using a foot-operated pedal and produces a deep thump when hit.

Hi-Hat Cymbals
The hi-hat is made up of two cymbals placed together and assembled onto a foot-operated stand. The hi-hat can be played in many fashions, closing the cymbals (by using the foot pedal) and hitting the top cymbal will be the main way we'll be playing the hi-hat throughout this book. Simply opening and closing the cymbals via the pedal is also common, along with hitting the top cymbal while the hi-hat is open. The hi-hat is used to keep time while playing rhythms and is very important to your kit.

Toms
You may find one or two toms mounted on top of your bass drum. These are called "rack" or "high toms." There are also floor toms, which are larger and are mounted independently on a stand of their own.

Cymbals
There are hundreds of splashes, crashes, rides, and other cymbals available, all of which serve a distinct purpose. Whether or not you have additional cymbals and drums than the ones mentioned above won't affect the usability of this book as we'll primarily focus on bass, snare, and hi-hat techniques. Many players start with only three pieces (snare, bass, and hi-hat) so that they can focus completely on the fundamentals before expanding.

Layout & Setup

The diagram will show you where all of your drums should be placed. The height of your drums is decided entirely by preference, so adjust it to your liking until you're comfortable.

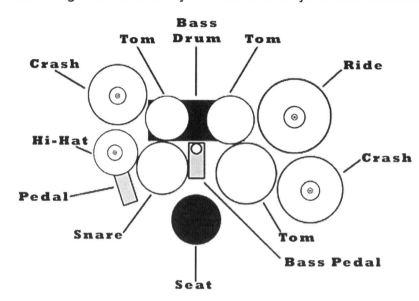

Seat Height

Your seat should be raised high enough so that your hip bone is above your knee (to avoid back pain). You should be at a comfortable height and still be able to fully place both feet on your pedals (left on hi-hat, right on bass).

Snare Drum

A general rule of thumb for your snare drum is to raise it just above knee height, or a couple inches below your belly button when seated. You may also choose to tilt the snare drum towards you slightly. When you sit, the snare should be in between your legs, but your thighs shouldn't hug the edges of the drum.

Floor Tom

The floor tom should be roughly the same height as your snare drum. You shouldn't have to turn around to play the floor tom, just rotate slightly at the hips to easily hit it.

Hi-hat

The hi-hat cymbals should be raised high enough so that your left stick can easily hit the snare whilst your right stick is keeping time on the hi-hat. You'll be doing a lot of playing crossed-over like this, so give your left stick plenty of room to hit the snare and rebound back. Although your left stick needs room, your right arm shouldn't have to be awkwardly raised in order to hit the hi-hat. If you have to lift your shoulder or bring your elbow up, your hi-hat is likely too high. A trick to deciding on the hi-hat height is to place your right elbow on the snare, right in the middle of the drum. If you keep your elbow there and grab the hi-hat stand, your hand should be right under the bell of the bottom cymbal.

Toms & Cymbals

From your seat, you should be able to comfortably and easily grab the cymbals with your hands; shoulder height is a good place to start with your cymbals. Many players put there rack toms at just about chest height, with them dramatically tilted towards them. No matter the height, a good way to check your distance from your drums is to sit down as if you were about to play, then see if you can place your palm in the middle of each drum, if you can't your too far.

Sticks

The sticks you use will have a huge effect on your tone and technique; take your time to try out many different pairs before settling for one.

Woods

Drum sticks are typically made using three types of wood: hickory, maple, and oak. The type of wood you choose will change how the stick feels in your hand when you hit the drum because the density of the wood will affect how the vibrations move through the stick. Maple is very light and absorbs a lot of the vibrations, meaning you'll feel the hits less in your hands. Hickory is the most common with decent energy absorption and a good amount of flexibility. Oak is the densest of the three, and you'll certainly be able to feel the vibrations in your hands, but it's also the least likely to break and the most durable.

Tips

There are two choices for tips: wood and nylon. Wood-tipped sticks are the most common, and the only real downfall of them is that there's a chance they'll chip after using them for a while. A Nylon tipped stick will have better rebound and sound great on cymbals. If you happen to be playing on an electric kit (that doesn't have real drum heads) you'll want to use nylon-tipped sticks to increase the rebound and avoid damaging your kit. Do beware that nylon tips can fall off of your sticks.

Sizes

The higher the number when picking drumsticks, the thicker the stick, for example: a size 2b stick is much larger than a 7a. Keep in mind that brands don't have the exact same sizing guidelines (a 5a in one brand might be slightly larger or smaller in another).

- 7a: The smaller the stick, the quieter the hit, this is why most jazz drummers go with thinner sticks (and some even use special brushes). A size 7a is thin, light, and is perfect for younger drummers.
- 5a: These are the most common to start with, and many stick with them. The medium thickness is very versatile and is perfect for rock drummers. You can play both loudly and softly without changing sticks.
- 2b/5b: Thicker than average, these are good for louder playing and perfectly suitable for heavy rock and metal playing.

Finishes

You should keep in mind that the different finishes (varnish and the like) will affect how the sticks feel and how well you can grip them. There are also many new designs coming out, some with rubber coatings and others colorful finishes. Be careful with colored sticks, as they could leave marks on cymbals and drums. Likewise, also be weary of rubber coatings that promise better grip and longer life. The rubber can be easily cut on the edges of cymbals and will also have a huge impact on the sound of your kit. Starting with traditional wooden sticks is likely the best way to go so that you can develop proper technique.

Matched Grip

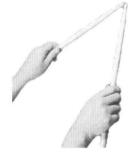

Keep these things in mind when holding your sticks. Go through the checklist each time when you sit down, and check your grip often (eventually, it'll become second nature with practice).

Throughout this book, keep in mind that you should always be hitting the center of the drum for the best sound and least wear on your drum heads.

- When holding your sticks, you need to remember to keep a loose grip. Holding your sticks too tight will lead to lack of rebound, bad technique, and the potential of injury. Hold one stick in each hand and put your hands out in front of you with your palms facing upwards, roll the sticks using your thumb and fingers. You'll notice that to roll the sticks around in your hands, you need an extremely loose grip, just enough so you don't drop them. This is about how lose you should always hold your sticks when playing.
- Don't hold your sticks at the very end, grip them about 2" up from the end to maximize rebound.
- When you go to hit the drums, keep your palms facing downwards, don't twist your wrists or arm.

There are many different grips, all of which produce different sounds and have different uses. For book 1, you should use this grip (referred to as "matched grip") to do all of your playing. It's perfect for everything we'll be learning and is applicable to all different styles.

Tuning

Before we start playing, we need to tune your kit. A few players tune their drums to notes, but it's a real hassle unless you have good pitch (the ability the recognize notes). For most players, simply tuning each drum so that it sounds good is an easier route. There are many tuners out there for drums, and you may consider picking one up so that you can get the best sound out of your kit. It's much easier to tune to notes if you have a tuner that clips onto the hoop of your drum to tell you the actual pitches.

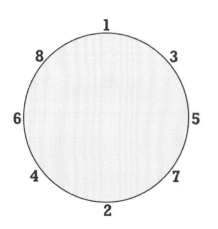

The quickest route, especially when you want to start playing as soon as possible, is to just focus on getting each individual drum sounding its best. When you put the drum heads onto your drum, tighten the lugs in a crisscross pattern (as pictured), turning each one an even amount of times. Repeat this process with each head on every drum until the wrinkles disappear. Continue to do this until you're satisfied with the sound produced when you hit the center of the top drumhead.

Basic Tuning

Use the tuning peg to hit the drum head next to each lug. At every lug, you should get the same pitch. If the pitch is too low, tighten the lug. If it's too high, loosen it. If your drums have an even amount of lugs, then it's likely lugs opposite one another will have the same pitch. Using the diagram from before, if you were to hit the lug numbered 1 and found the pitch was higher than the others; it's likely that the lug numbered 2 would also be higher. Tuning the drum head to itself using the crisscross pattern is likely the best way to tune your drums for the first time. If a pitch is too low for your liking, bring it up, and bring down the higher pitches until everything meets in the middle. Like many aspects of drumming, the tuning of each drum is based on your personal preference.

Seating Heads

When you first put the drumheads on, then tune them to pitch, you'll likely need to seat the head. Do this by placing your palm on the center on the head and pressing down, not too hard, just enough to push the head into place. You may hear a cracking sound when you do this, but don't let that alarm you. Once you seat the head, check the drum's tuning, as it may have dropped significantly in pitch. If that's the case, the head needed to be seated. Now, repeat the tuning process, then seat the head again until the pitch stays the same. Usually, you can safely seat all the heads on your drums, top and bottom, except for the snare drum. Never press directly on the bottom head of a snare, as it's extremely thin (the majority of them are about the thickness of kitchen plastic wrap).

Tuning Cymbals

You may hear people talk about "tuning cymbals" but there is really no way to tune a cymbal. There is nothing to tighten or loosen, as it's just a single piece of material. What most people mean when they talk about cymbal tuning is tweaking the sound of the cymbal. There are special tapes you can place onto cymbals to slightly change the tones they produce, but this isn't technically tuning, just altering.

Muffling & Adjusting Drums

If your drums are too loud, you may try placing pillows inside (most commonly the bass drum). Some players take the front head off of the bass drum completely, and sometimes even the bottom heads of the toms. These are all useable solutions to muffling and silencing drums, but you may also want to consider getting a mesh-head conversion kit. You'll have the same rebound as real drum heads, but you won't have to worry about silencing. Some kits will also convert your acoustic into an electric, so you can still hear the sounds.

You may notice that if you play your bass drum, your toms ring, or if you hit a cymbal, your snare rattles. Little unwanted vibrations like these are normal, but there are many products out there that will help prevent the unwanted sounds, like damper rings, gels, and tape, but sometimes you just need to adjust the drums themselves. Snare drums have a couple adjustments for the snares that you can mess with. You can also try retuning the snare and bass, or repositioning the drums so that they're not as close.

Planning Your Practice

In order to get the most out of your practice sessions, you need to plan them ahead of time. Practice time and jam time shouldn't be confused with each other. Practice time is when you work on the technical aspects of your playing to become a better drummer. Jam time is when you apply those techniques to your playing by practicing along to music or learning a new song. It's important to break up your practice time and your jam time. Make sure you know what you'll be working on before sitting down. Planning your practice the night before or even a week ahead will make sure you don't waste time "noodling" which could instead be better spent practicing. Noodling around on your kit, that is, randomly playing beats and goofing off, is important to being able to create fills, but you need to avoid doing it until you've worked on everything that you needed to.

Here are some tips to get the most out of your sessions:

- Plan ahead. Decide how much time you have and what exactly you need to be doing.
- Set goals for yourself, and make them specific. Maybe you're trying to play the backbeat at 120 bpm.
- Always use a metronome, as a drummer, timing is everything.
- When you're done practicing, mess around on your kit and have fun.
- Don't get frustrated if you can't play something, and certainly don't take out your frustration by playing harder. This can lead to injury and bad habits.
- It's very important to stay relaxed when you play, don't grip the sticks too tight and don't get into the habit of clenching your teeth or locking your elbows.

The main things you should focus on when just starting to play is stick technique (your grip and how you strike), your timing (metronomes are extremely important), and reading drum notation. Once you have these things down, you'll be able to play faster and better, but it will take a good amount of practice. When you go to learn songs, start slow. Don't try to play a new beat full-speed before you can even play it at half. Start with 25% speed, then work your way up from there. If the song is at 120 bpm, start at 30 bpm until you can play it correctly and easily. Playing slow can be harder than playing fast, even if you can play a beat at full-speed, challenge yourself to slow it down and really focus on your technique; it will help you become a better drummer.

Lastly, don't overlook the details when learning a piece. You'll find that many classic songs have tiny nuances that change the sound of the piece entirely. If you listen to AC/DC's "Back in Black" you'll probably hear a familiar beat. It's a variation of the backbeat, but Phil Rudd doesn't play the hi-hat as you typically would; he alternates between hitting the shoulder and striking normally. Little changes like this one can be hard to play and may seem pointless, but if you play that song just striking normally, you'll find that it sounds repetitive, much like a drum machine.

Keep these things in mind whenever you sit down to practice.

Drum Notation I

Drum notation shows you both the rhythm and which pieces you should be playing. Let's start with the hi-hat. Put your foot onto the pedal and close the cymbals together tightly. Hold one stick in your right hand (assuming you write with your right-hand and have set everything up as illustrated on page 7). We're going to play quarter notes on the hi-hat; all you have to do is count "1 and 2 and 3 and 4 and" and hit the hi-hat on each number. Hit the middle of the top cymbal, not the edge. The edge is considered the shoulder, and the bell is the raised part in the center where the pole of the stand is. You should be hitting the hi-hat in-between the shoulder and the bell with the tip of your stick. Here are quarter notes on the hi-hat (exactly what you're playing):

As you count "1 and 2 and 3 and 4 and" also start hitting the hi-hat on the "and" after each number. Now you're playing eighth notes, which are twice as fast as the quarter notes we were playing before. On drum notation, eighth notes on the hi-hat looks like this:

 Notice the eighth notes are beamed together. This is because individual eighth notes have flags; when there are multiple eighth notes in a measure, we beam them for easier reading. Notice that the single flag turns into a single beam.

Now that you can play eighth notes on the hi-hat, we can add in other pieces of the kit. Continue counting as you play the eighth notes with your right hand. When you say "two" and "four" hit the snare drum with your left hand. That looks like this:

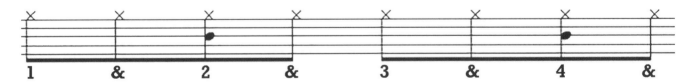

Keep practicing this part until you have your hand coordination down. You should be hitting the snare drum right on time. Keep counting (it's best to do it out loud) as you play. Start slow, then build up speed, making sure that you aren't hitting the shoulder of the hi-hat and that you're keeping a loose grip. Hit the drum in the center and watch your hands.

Backbeat

Once you're comfortable playing the snare and hi-hat together, you can add in the bass drum. Keeping the same rhythm as before, eighth notes on the hi-hat and the snare on beats two and four, you can add the bass drum on beats one and three. Here's how that looks in drum notation:

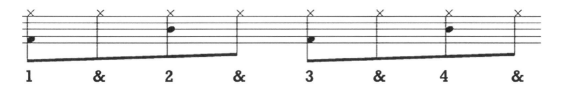

This is known as the backbeat, and it's a basic rhythm used in thousands of songs of all styles, prominently rock. Don't get frustrated if you find yourself playing the bass drum off time. Getting the timing and coordination down can be tough, practice this beat each day until you can play it fast and slow. Try counting and playing each piece individually, then adding in and taking out things while you play. Most importantly, even if you make a mistake, don't stop playing. Continuously play the eighth notes on the hi-hat, even if you hit the bass or snare off time, don't stop, just keep counting and try again on beat 1. Once you're able to easily play the backbeat, you'll find all of the variations that we'll be learning surprisingly easy.

Since the backbeat is used in so many songs, there's a good chance you can find one on your playlist and drum along. Listen for the tempo and start with the hi-hat. Once you have the speed down, add in the bass and snare. You'll hear if you're playing off time. The drum you'll likely hear stand out in the song is the snare, so you'll easily be able to locate beats two and four. Tom Petty and AC/DC songs are a great place to start practicing the backbeat.

Metronomes

Metronomes are very important to help you improve your timing. There are many mobile applications and affordable metronomes that will work well enough for your practice sessions. A metronome keeps time for you. It clicks at a constant rate that you set in order to ensure you don't speed up or slow down without realizing it.

The BPM (beats per minute) is typically measured in quarter notes. So if you set a metronome to 60 bpm, it'll play 60 clicks a minute. Each time you hear the click, you should be counting out a number and saying the "and" in-between the clicks. Sometimes playing slow is tougher than playing fast, so try practicing at all different speeds. Keep in mind that your technique is more important than how quickly you can play a beat, always focus on your grip and positioning more than the speed of the metronome.

An important note: BPM and tempo is the same thing, both refer to the speed of a song.

Warm-ups

Getting your strokes even can be a tough job for many drummers. There are many snare drum exercises to help strengthen your weak hand and improve your technique.

Singles

Singles are played by hitting the drum once with each hand repeatedly, like so ("R" is for right stick, "L" is for left stick):

This is a measure of sixteenth notes, which are twice as fast as eighth notes. They're counted out as: "1 e and ah 2 e and ah 3 e and ah 4 e and ah." Notice that if you just count the numbers "1 2 3 4" those are quarter notes. If you divide those in half, you're playing eighth notes: "1 and 2 and 3 and 4 and." If you cut the eighth notes in half, you get the sixteenth notes "1 e and ah 2 e and ah 3 e and ah 4 e and ah." With the counting, here's how the above measure looks:

 Notice that sixteenth notes have two beams. This is because an individual sixteenth note has two flags (just like the single eighth note flag turned into a single beam). When you connect notes the flags they turn into beams.

As you practice this, remember to count out loud. Using a metronome will help you stay on time. Check your grip, and make sure you're hitting the drum directly in the center. Your goal is for both hands to hit the drum evenly, meaning that no matter which hand you're using, both strokes sound out at the same volume with the same sound. Working on even strokes will take a lot of practice. Many players invest in practice pads, which are small, silent and portable products that have the same rebound of a drum, but you can practice with them whenever and wherever.

Rebound

When you hit the drum, your stick should bounce back up. This is known as rebound. You shouldn't have to force down every single stroke. As you start to play, your sticks should rebound back up, and then land on the drum again with little effort on your part. This process should keep repeating. Both sticks should be rebounding up the same amount, about chin height. All you really need to do is guide the sticks to the center by keeping a loose grip and good position. This is how you get strong, even strokes. Remember these tips when you practice any of the beats in this book.

Doubles

To play doubles hit the drum twice, then switch hands. Here are sixteenth note doubles:

| R | R | L | L | R | R | L | L | R | R | L | L | R | R | L | L |

Starting any of these exercises with your weaker hand will help improve your technique. You can apply these exercises to any drum or cymbal. If you have a double bass drum (either a double pedal or two bass drums) you can also apply these to your feet.

Stick Exercises

Here are more warm-ups you can do on the snare drum. They're written as eighth notes, but you should also play the patterns as sixteenth notes. Focus on getting good rebound, even volume, and keeping a loose grip. You should spend at least ten minutes a day warming up with these exercises. It will improve your technique and counting abilities.

1	and	2	and	3	and	4	and
L	L	L	L	L	L	L	L
R	R	R	R	R	R	R	R
L	L	L	L	R	R	R	R
L	R	L	R	L	L	R	R
L	L	R	L	L	L	R	L
R	L	R	R	R	L	R	L
R	L	R	L	R	R	L	R
L	L	R	R	R	R	L	L
R	L	L	R	L	L	R	L

The below patterns start as eight notes, then speed up into sixteenth notes:

1	and	2	and	3	e	and	ah	4	e	and	ah
L	L	L	L	L	R	L	R	L	R	L	R
R	R	R	R	R	L	R	L	R	L	R	L
L	L	R	R	L	L	R	L	R	L	L	R

Repeat all of these patterns at least twice through, without stopping.

Basic Beats

These beats use the same hi-hat and snare pattern that you learned on page 12. The only thing differing between these rhythms is when the bass drum is played. All of these rhythms are used by professional musicians and it's worth memorizing a few.

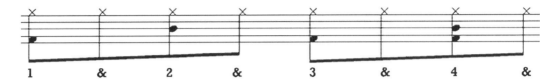

Notice that the above rhythm is the same as the backbeat (page 13) except you add the bass drum on beat four.

You should realize that the beam can be connecting the notes on the top or the bottom. The direction of flags and beams depends on space and preference; it doesn't change anything other than appearance.

As you get more advanced, you can also try playing sixteenth notes on the hi-hat.

Here are more variations to practice with (repeat each one at least twice):

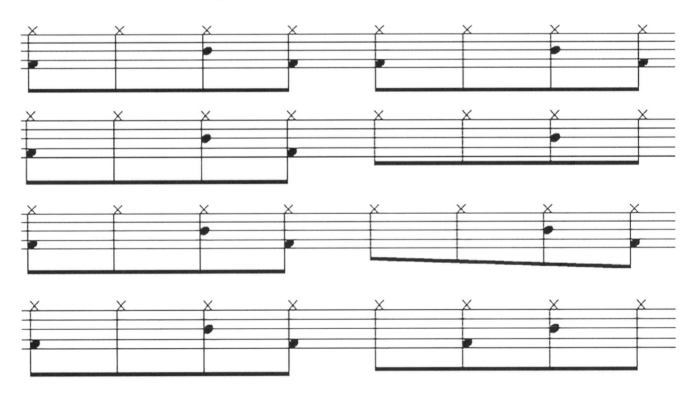

Drum Notation II

Note Durations

whole   half quarter eighth sixteenth

The diagram to the left is showing the five most common note durations. In common time (4/4) a whole note lasts four beats, a half note two beats, a quarter note 1 beat, and so on. So far, we've played using quarter, eighth, and sixteenth notes in our rhythms.

Counting Rhythms

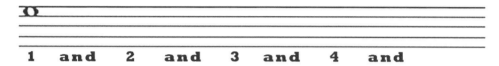

A whole note lasts for the count of four beats.

Half notes last for two beats, half the duration of a whole note.

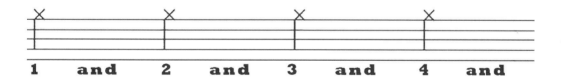

Quarter notes last for one beat, half the duration of a half note.

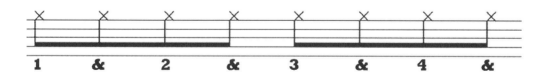

Eighth notes last for ½ beat, half the duration of quarter notes.

Sixteenth notes last for ¼ beat, half the duration of an eighth note.

Beams & Flags

Eighth notes appear as quarter notes with a single flag, and sixteenth notes appear as quarter notes with two flags. When you beam notes together, you can determine the type of note by counting the beams. The number of beams always corresponds to the number of flags on the individual note, for example: eighth notes (one flag) beamed together will use one beam. Similarly, sixteenth notes (two flags) will have two beams when connected. The beams may be connecting the notes on top, or on the bottom, this has no effect on the duration of the notes and only changes the appearance.

Stems

Notes without flags (whole, half, and quarter notes) may be written without stems attached. The stem is the line extending from the note on which the flags of eighth and sixteenth notes are connected to. Whether or not a note has a stem attached, and whether it's pointing up or down, will not affect the duration of the note in anyway.

Eighth and Sixteenth Notes

You can connect eighth and sixteenth notes in the same group, like so:

This awkward grouping can be hard to play. Rhythms like this one can get tricky. It's best to write it down, count it out, and double check your work. Sometimes, it helps to count out the entire measure using the smallest duration you're working with. For example, since our smallest notes are sixteenth notes, we can write in the counting for a complete measure of sixteenth notes to help us decide how long each note lasts:

Remember these things to help you:

1. Eight notes last twice as long as a sixteenth note, so they get two counts ("1 e").
2. Quarter notes last four times as long, so they get four counts ("4 e and a").
3. Pay less attention to what you're writing (whether it's a number, letter, or otherwise) and instead count how many of each that you're writing until you figure out all of the durations.

18

Notation Key

The first tom is the tom that is highest in pitch (and smallest in size) if you have two rack toms, it will be the one on the left. (known as the high-tom) The second tom will be lower in pitch (and larger) and should be mounted to the right of tom 1 (this is the mid-tom). The floor tom is the largest of the three and deepest in pitch (known as the low-tom). The bass drum can be thought of as a giant tom on it's side, and is therefore located on the bottom space of the staff.

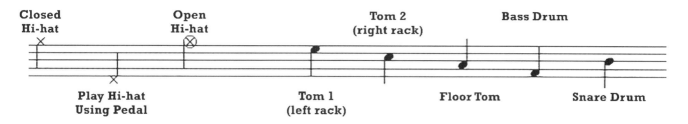

The above measure will show you where the main pieces of your set will show up on standard drum notation.

Variations

Unfortunately, there isn't complete uniformity to these standards. You may occasionally see the pieces notated slightly differently, but throughout all Lutz Academy drumming books, we'll use the above methods.

Staff

Music staff is what we've been using so far to notate our rhythms and patterns. It's made up of five lines and four spaces. The vertical placement of a note, along with the appearance, will help you know which part of the kit you should be playing, and how long the note should last.

Staff is broken up into measures using vertical lines, called "barlines." Measures (or "bars") help us keep track of time. A single barline separates measures, a double barline usually ends a section, and a

terminal barline ends the piece or song.

When you need to repeat a measure, you'll see the repeat signs pictured below. You should repeat everything in between the two signs. How many times you should repeat the measure will be written above the staff. If there is no specified number, assume you should only repeat it once.

Time Signatures

 The time signature is shown at the beginning of the first measure in a song. It's shown as a fraction, like 4/4. 4/4 tells you that there are four beats in a measure and that a quarter note (worth 1/4) gets one beat. 4/4 is considered common time, and may also be represented with a "C."

6/8 time means there are six beats in each measure, and an eighth note (1/8) gets one beat. Similarly, in 3/4 time there are three beats per measure, and a quarter note (1/4) gets one beat.

Rests

whole   half   quarter   eighth   sixteenth

Rests tell you how long to wait before playing the next note. All rests are equal to the notes of the same name, meaning a whole rest last four beats, a half rest lasts two beats, a quarter rest lasts one beat, an eighth rests last ½ beat, and a sixteenth rest lasts ¼ beat.

Drum Tablature

Drum tablature is a common form of notation. It's fairly simple to read. The pieces of your kit are abbreviated at the beginning of the piece, like so:

```
H  |----------------|  Hi-hat
t  |----------------|  Small Tom
T  |----------------|  Mid/Medium Tom
S  |----------------|  Snare Drum
F  |----------------|  Floor Tom
B  |----------------|  Bass Drum
Hf |----------------|  Hi-hat with Foot
```

As you can see, the order of the pieces follows the same order as the notes on staff do. For example, the top line represents the hi-hat, just like the hi-hat is represented in a space at the top of the staff. The small tom is on the line below the hi-hat, just like it's below the hi-hat on staff.

Here's the basic notation for hitting drums:
|-o-| Strike Drum
|-O-| Accent (hit harder)

Here's the basic notation for playing cymbals:
|-x-| Strike Cymbal
|-o-| Open Hi-hat
|-#-| Choke Cymbal (grab the edge after playing to mute it)
|-b-| Play the Bell
|-x-| Click Hi-hat using Pedal

We'll explain more on using these techniques later, for now, you just need to be able to recognize them. Here's an example of drum tablature employing some of these techniques:

```
H  |---o-------------|   Here, we're playing the open hi-hat, then
t  |-----------------|   clicking it by closing it with the foot pedal.
T  |-----------------|   To end the piece, we're playing the snare drum.
S  |--------------o--|   We don't actually need to include the other pieces of the kit
F  |-----------------|   since we're not using any of the them. You'll likely see tab
B  |-----------------|   written using only the pieces that are played within that song
Hf |-----------x-----|   or measure.
```

Rhythm in drum tablature is counted beneath the tab, like so:

```
H  |------------------------------|
t  |------------------------------|
S  |------------------------------|
B  |------------------------------|
   |1 e + a 2 e + a 3 e + a 4 e + a|
```

Repeats are written above the tab, using one of these methods:

```
   |----------repeat 4x-------|
H  |------------|------------|
S  |------------|------------|
B  |------------|------------|
   |1t12t13t14t1|1t12t13t14t1|
```

```
   |---------play 4x---------|
H  |------------|------------|
S  |------------|------------|
B  |------------|------------|
   |1t12t13t14t1|1t12t13t14t1|
```

```
   |========= 4x ===========|
H  |------------|------------|
S  |------------|------------|
B  |------------|------------|
   |1t12t13t14t1|1t12t13t14t1|
```

All of the above measures are telling you to repeat the piece four times. Other pieces you may find in tab are:

```
C  |-----------------|   Cymbal
Rd |-----------------|   Ride Cymbal
F2 |-----------------|   2nd Floor Tom
```

Learning and practicing your notation reading skills will make learning songs much easier. You have to know how to properly interpret rhythms and be able to recreate the written notes on your kit. Having good sight-reading skills will take a lot of practice. You should incorporate music reading into your practice sessions just like you will technique work and song practice.

Techniques

Basic Drum Strokes

Full Stroke	Down Stroke	Up Stroke	Tap Stroke

Start in up position, end in up position	Start in up position, end in down position.	Start in down position, end in up position.	Start in down position, end in down position.

The above graphics represent where your stick should be at the end of each stroke. Up position can be seen in the first photo and down position can be seen in the second photo.

Stroke Practice

Practice your strokes by playing a full, down, tap, and up stroke with your right hand, then alternate to your left. You may find getting a practice pad helpful so that you can practice away from your set. While you're watching television and doing similar activities you can use practice pads to silently be improving your technique. When you're listening to music, practice your strokes. The song will act as a metronome and make practicing more fun.

Multiple Bounce Roll

Also called a "buzz roll," the multiple bounce roll is accomplished by playing a down stroke once, then allowing the stick to bounce, creating a roll. You want to practice this roll with each hand individually. Your goal is for a single hit to give rapid, smooth bounces that last. If you find that your stick stops bouncing after two or three times, check your grip. Hitting the center of the drum with just the right amount of force will give sustainable and quick bounces. If you don't press hard enough, the stick will stop after a few bounces. If you press too hard into the head, the stick won't bounce at all. Try making your buzz roll last, then alternate hands as it nears the end. Your goal is to get a smooth roll effect as you continuously alternate between hands.

Flams

A flam uses both your sticks. You'll hit the drum one right after the other. Play an up stroke with one hand as you play a down stroke with the other. They shouldn't be hitting the drum at the same time. A right flam is played by playing an up stroke with your left hand, and a down stroke with your right. A left flam is accomplished by playing an up stroke with your right hand and a down stroke with your left.

Hi-Hat Splash & Clicking

A splash gives a sound similar to striking a crash cymbal and is done by stomping on the pedal, then quickly letting back up. A click is done by pressing on the pedal to close the cymbals, then opening them again (producing a clicking like sound).

Rhythm Counting

Eighth Note Patterns

The following beats use whole, half, quarter, and eighth note rests and patterns. Some measures are counted out for you. While the patterns are written using the bass drum, you can (and should) practice them on the hi-hat, snare, and other drums. You can also try playing the rhythms using multiple different pieces.

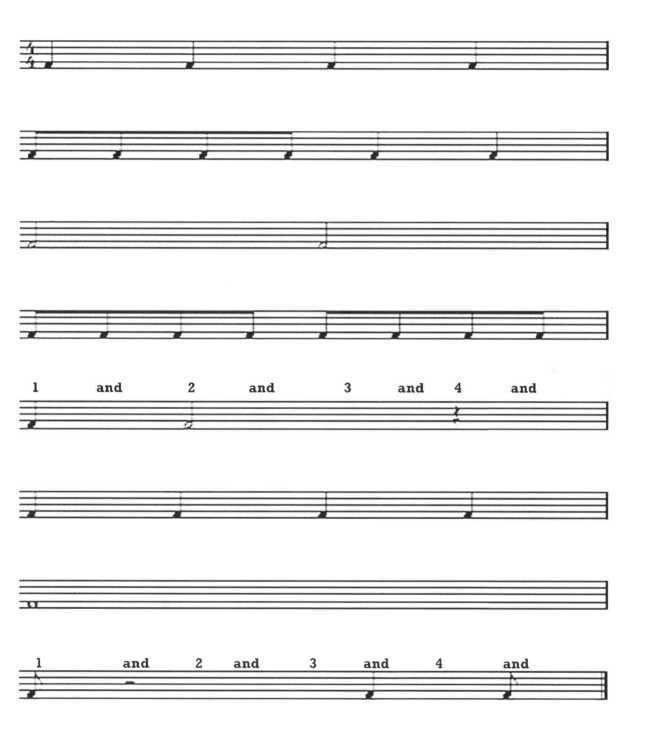

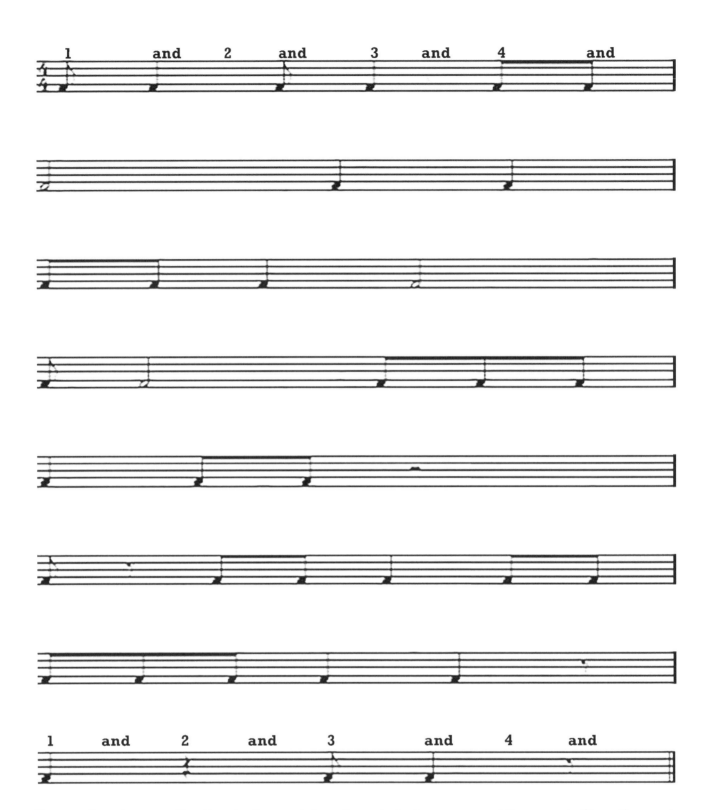

Remember to pay attention to the rest durations to help you count these out. Counting out loud as you play will help you stay on time. Use a metronome and start at 60pm, then gradually speed up the tempo. Look a few notes ahead as you play to keep you on track. Try writing out some odd rhythms of your own and practice with them. Most importantly, don't memorize these exercises. You want to work on your sight-reading abilities, not your memorization skills!

Sixteenth Note Patterns

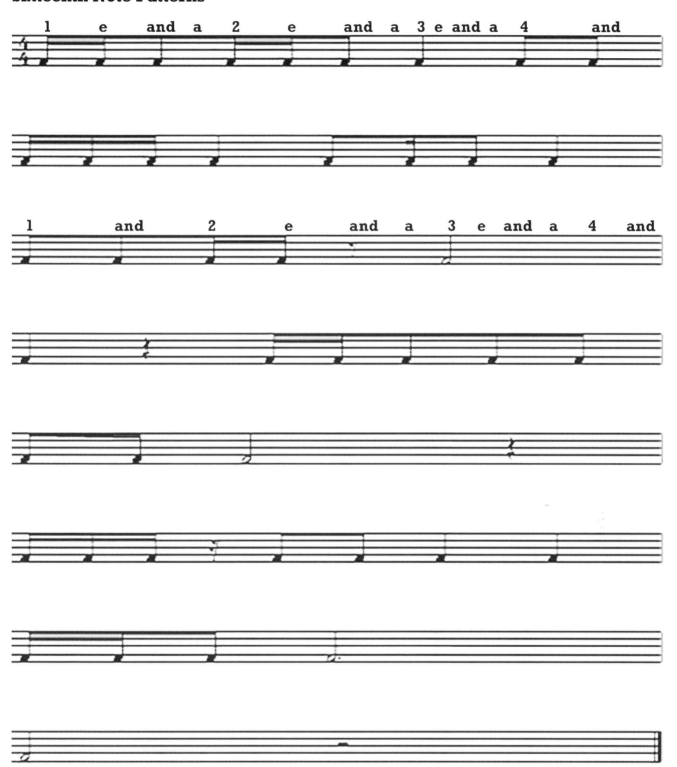

In the 7th measure, the above rhythm has a dotted half note. A dot next to a note adds half of its value (it makes the note last 1.5x its length), so this half note lasts for 2 beats (half note) plus half of that (1 beat), meaning it has a total value of three beats.

You may find measure two especially difficult to play. This measure alternates between eighth and sixteenth notes, which can be tricky to count and even more awkward to play, being able to work through tough rhythms like this one will help improve your rhythm counting skills. If you're having a hard time with a rhythm, count it out on a separate piece of paper. Try to avoid writing rhythm counts in this book; your goal is to be able to play these on the spot without memorizing.

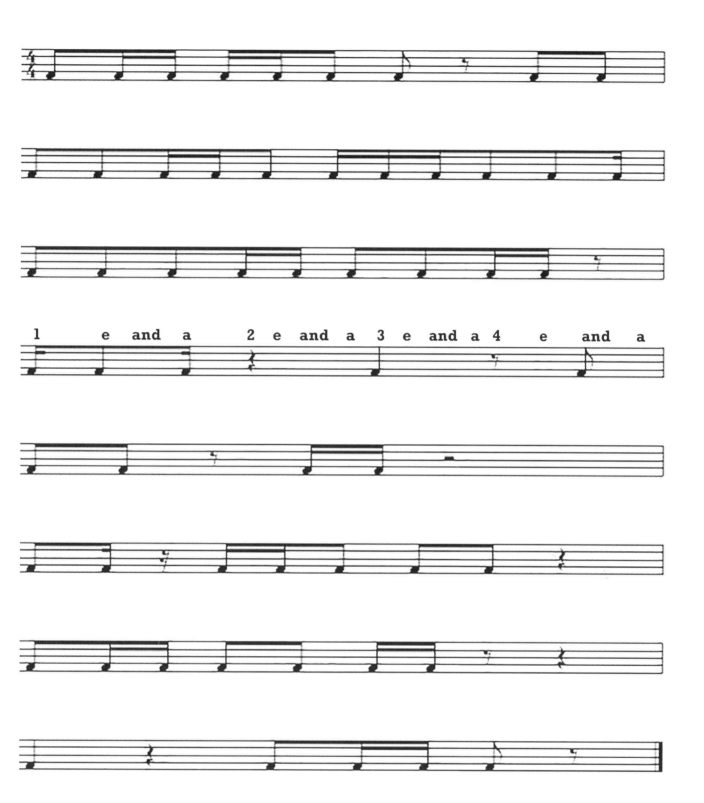

When dealing with a lot of rests, you need to keep counting (either out loud or silently) along with the metronome while tapping your foot in order to keep proper time. Hearing yourself count aloud whilst listening to the metronome click and actively hitting the hi-hat (or continuously tapping your foot) will really help improve your sense of time and how well you can keep track of rhythms.

Changing Time Signatures

The following rhythm counting exercises employ different time signatures.

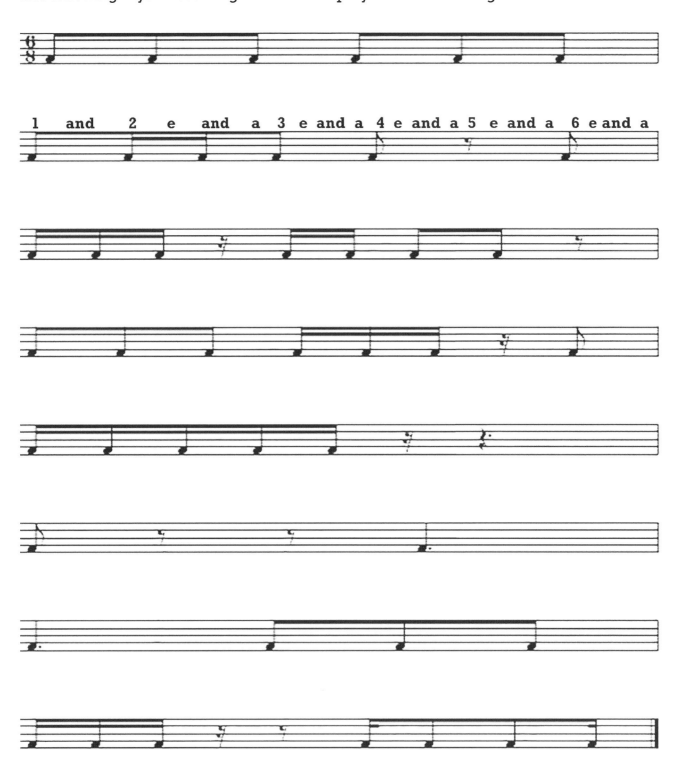

1   and   2   e   and   a   3 e and a   4 e and a   5 e and a   6 e and a

According to our time signature (6/8) an eighth note gets 1 beat ("1 and") and there are six beats in a measure. In 4/4 (common time) a quarter note usually gets 1 beat, so you can now think of eighth notes as quarter notes, sixteenth notes as eighth notes, and so on (meaning the quarter notes last the length of a half note).

28

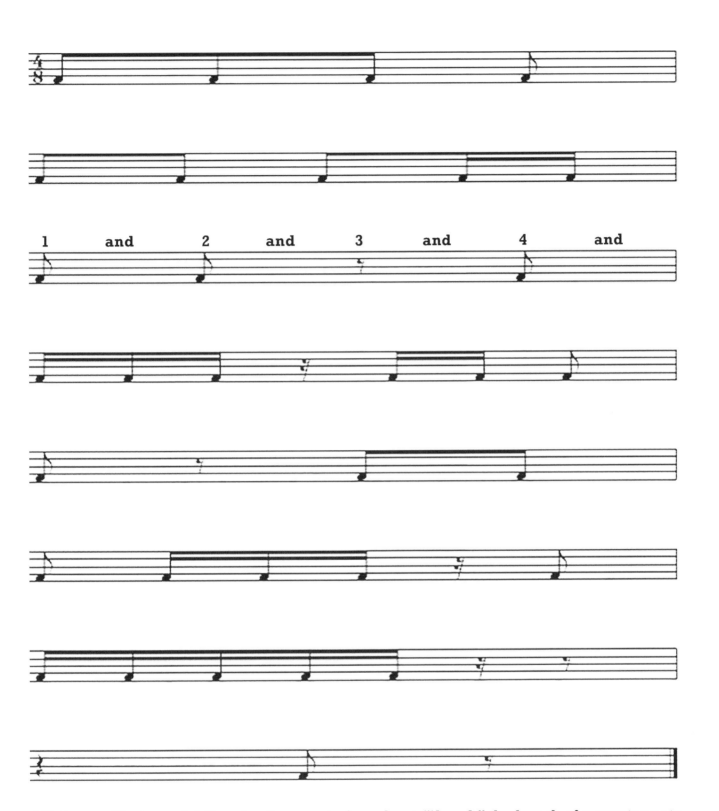

4/8 times still gives eighth notes the count of one beat ("1 and," the length of a quarter note in common time), but there are only four beats in a measure, like we're used to.

Another common time signature you'll run into is half of common time, or 2/2 time (just like 4/4 time is represented with a "C" on occasion, 2/2 time may be represented with a "C" that has a line down the center).

In 8/2 time, there are eight beats in a measure and a half note gets one beat. This means quarter notes are worth 1/2 beat (the length of an eighth note in common time), eighth notes are worth 1/4 beat (the length of a sixteenth note in common time), and sixteenth notes are worth 1/8 beat (the length of a 32nd note in common time, half of a sixteenth note). 32nd notes are too fast to count so we group them to keep track. Two 32nd notes equal a sixteenth note; four 32nd notes equal an eighth note, and so on.

Thirty-Second Note Patterns

In measure three, we have two 32nd notes, which we'll count as "2" (because two 32nd notes equal one sixteenth note). 32nd notes and smaller divisions are uncommon due to the fact that they're hard to count and tough to play. While you should know how to play and recognize them, don't worry too much about having to deal with them on a regular basis.

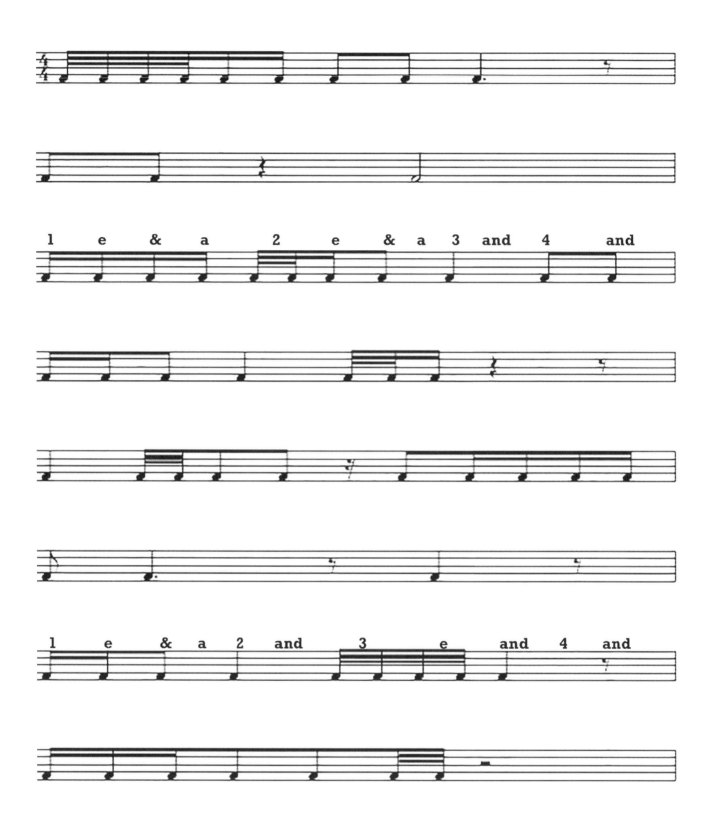

In measure 7, we have four 32nd notes which can be counted as a group. Four 32nd notes equal an eighth note, so we'll count it as "3 e." Remember to space these notes evenly. Setting the tempo very slow we'll help you when practicing 32nd notes.

A 32nd note rest will appear with three flags, just likc an individual 32nd note.

Beats

On the following pages you'll find 100+ classic beats, practice a few each day, along with fills (page 47), rhythm counting (page 23), and your technique. On page 51, you'll find expert tips and tricks to help improve your playing.

When playing any of these beats, here are some important things to remember:

1. Use a metronome.
2. Start slow (about 60-80bpm) and build up speed (120-160bpm).
3. When you speed up the tempo, don't let your technique suffer. Slowly bump up the speed until you can play quickly *and* correctly.
4. Count out loud and listen for the metronome as you play.
5. Keep a loose grip with your palms facing down.
6. Make sure you're getting good rebound on the snare with your left hand.
7. Practice songs as well as these beats. While you do need to focus on the technical aspects of your playing, you also need to learn how to apply it with songs.
8. Instead of using a metronome, play your favorite songs and drum-along.
9. Play these beats using your own variations. Try playing sixteenth notes on the hi-hat while keeping everything else the same. You could also switch drums (i.e. use the ride instead of the hi-hat, play a tom instead of the snare, etc.).
10. If you get frustrated, take a short break and come back when you're excited to learn again.
11. It can be tough working on your coordination, grip, and technique all at once, set aside some time each day to work on each one individually. Within a few weeks, you'll be better and faster, it just takes practice.
12. If you find yourself breaking sticks a lot, you need to check you're grip and positioning. This isn't something you should be doing frequently. Make sure you're hitting the drums in the center, that the side of your stick isn't hitting the rim, and that you're not striking too hard.
13. You may find that sometimes, you just don't have the motivation to practice. Many renowned players will recommend listening to a new band or song, watching a live performance, or finding someone to jam with in order to give you inspiration.
14. Once you have the basics down and can play some songs confidently, you might consider helping another beginner. The best way to learn something is to try and teach it. Show them some of the beats you've learned, and be another pair of eyes (and ears) for them to make sure they're gripping correctly and playing on time.
15. Have fun! We all start somewhere; just remember that you have to practice in order to get better. Write down how fast you can play certain beats each day in order to keep track of your progress. In a few weeks, you'll be surprised at how much better you've become with just an hour of daily practice.

Backbeat Variations

In addition to the variations mentioned before, you can also try opening and closing the hi-hat cymbals while you play. For example, play the hi-hat open on every number, and closed on the "and." This will improve your coordination and give you more variations.

34

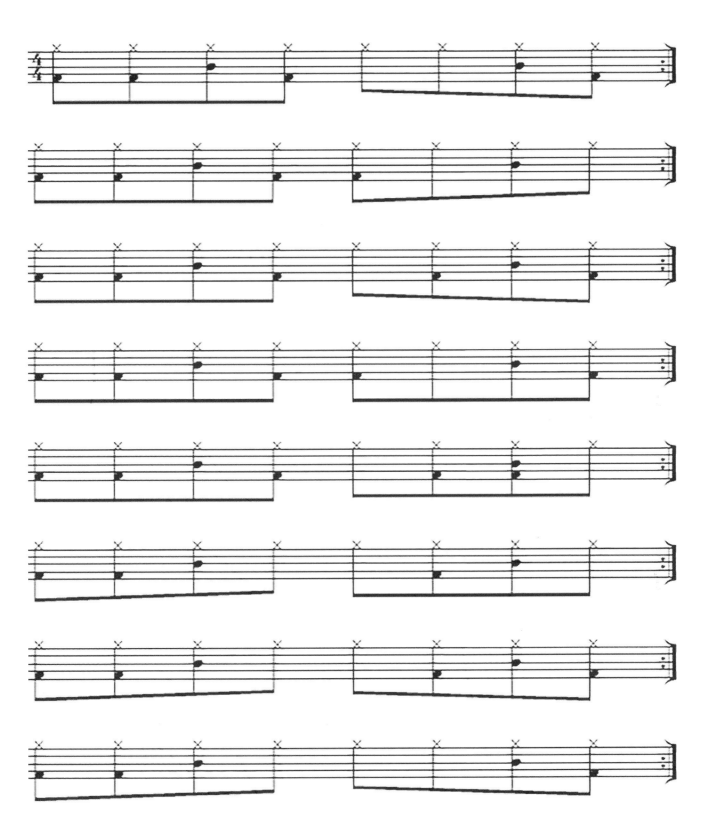

Try playing all of these beats in succession without stopping. Remember to keep playing the eighth notes on the hi-hat, even if you make a mistake.

If you find a specific beat hard to play, count it out first without playing, then try it slowly.

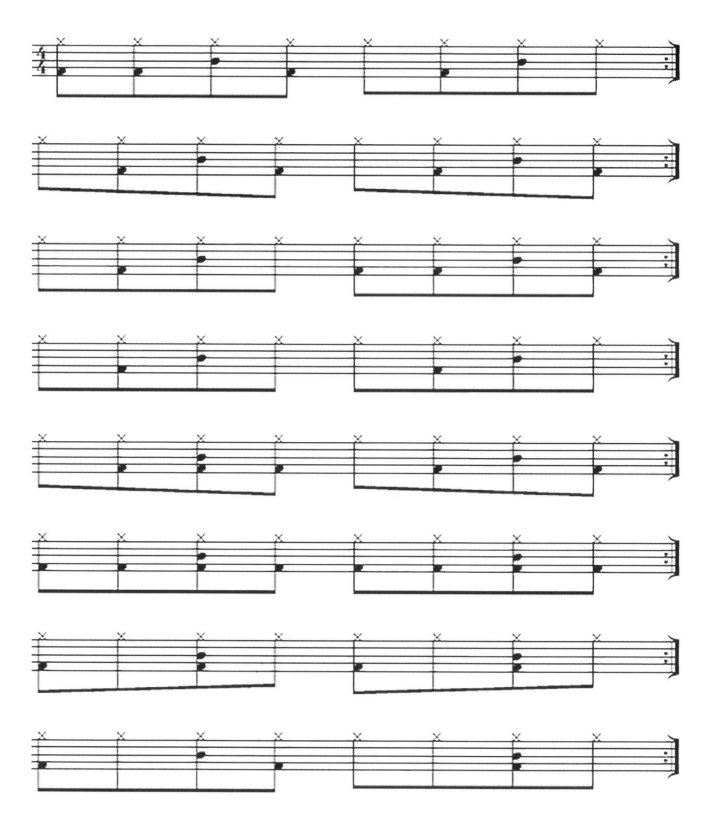

Instead of playing the hi-hat with your right hand, try clicking it using your foot instead. This will improve coordination as well as helping you develop your hi-hat technique. There are many different sounds that you can get out of the hi-hat; just changing where you strike (shoulder, bell, etc.) and how tightly the cymbals are closed will give you more sounds.

Two-Measure Beats

Once you practice some of these rhythms as they're written, you should switch up some of the pieces so you don't get tired of playing the same variations over and over again. You might try swapping the hi-hat with a cymbal, or playing the floor tom instead of the snare.

Find a rhythm that you particularly like, and memorize it so that as you play, you can focus on your hands instead of looking at the pages. Once you have it memorized, you can change some of it up and make it your own. This will help improve your creativity and explore the sounds of your kit.

Sixteenth Note Rhythms

The following rhythms incorporate sixteenth notes.

Count these patterns out loud before you try playing them

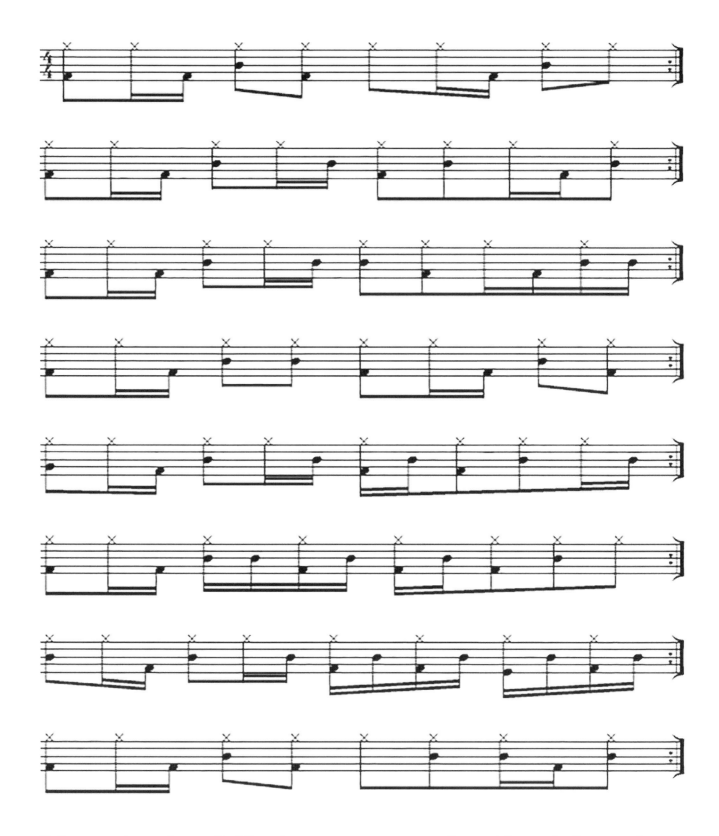

Before you try and use all of the pieces at once, you can clap out these rhythms or play them on a single drum or cymbal to help you get the feel for them.

Counting each measure out will help you make sure you're playing them correctly.

Remember, if you're having trouble playing these; review the rhythm counting exercises starting on page 23. You should write some of the rhythms out, count them aloud, and clap them to help you hear how it should sound.

Make sure to learn plenty of songs as you practice these beats.

Playing songs is the only way to apply what you're learning (other than writing music). There are thousands of lessons to be found online. If you end up using drum tablature, double check it's accuracy. If something seems wrong, play it how you think it should sound (always trust your ears).

As well as learning these rhythms, many beginner drummers challenge themselves to learn one song beat or fill each day (not the entire song, just a few measures). This will give you more ideas and increase your abilities. Write down the parts you learn in a notebook to track your progress as you learn new things.

If you're trying to learn a complete song, learn the hardest part first. It will make the rest of the song easier to learn and you'll learn the piece faster. Slow down everything, even if you think you can play it full-speed. If you practice and learn it sloppy, you'll only be able to play it that way.

Keep in mind that whatever beats you learn to play can be applied to multiple aspects of your playing. You can use these beats as a basis for song-writing, or use them to improve your overall ability. Many songs use the beats that you're learning, it's a possibility you've already heard a few of them in your favorite songs.

Come back to these beats every day and practice them. Even if you spend just 15 minutes working on some tough beats, you'll still be building speed, bettering your sight-reading ability, and improving your technique.

There are over 100 beats here, switch up the ones that you practice each day so you don't get bored.

Fills

Fills have many uses, their commonly played to signal the next section of a song or to cue a band mate to play their part. You may also use fills to begin a song, end a piece, or buildup a solo.

Eighth Note Fills

As you can see, the above fills use basic eighth note patterns. No cymbals (other than the hi-hat for the backbeat) are used, it's just your snare, toms, and bass drum.

A common variation of these fills is to play it (as written), then hit your crash cymbal on the 1 of the next measure. You can also try incorporating short rolls on each drum as you hit them and adding in cymbals to the patterns. You should think of these fills and beats as templates that you can change to your liking. Practice changing the rhythms, tempos, and pieces and you'll find a lot more opportunities in these basic fills than you otherwise would.

Broken Eighth Note Fills

These fills use rests and eighth notes.

These broken eighth note fills are slightly more advanced than the basic eighth note fills on the previous page. You should start learning these fills at about 60bpm, and then increase it as you get more comfortable. A good goal is 120bpm for all of these beats and fills, being able to play them quickly without harming your technique will take some practice. Learning beats and fills can take a lot of practice, and there's a lot to worry about when you're first starting to play. You may find it helpful to get a friend or fellow drummer to watch you practice. They can help you make sure that you're playing on time, holding your sticks properly, and correctly playing the beats.

Once you have these eighth note fills mastered, you should learn the sixteenth note fills on the following pages. Before moving on, you should practice applying these beats and fills to songs. You can find drum-less backing tracks online to play along to.

Sixteenth Note Fills

These sixteenth note fills are more advanced than the eighth note ones we learned previously. You should take the time to practice them all before moving on to the broken sixteenth note fills on the next page.

As you practice, you'll find that you can play more complicated things more quickly and easily. While it can be frustrating when you're first starting out, taking the time to learn the fundamentals correctly will make everything else much easier.

Make sure to take breaks when you get frustrated, but don't walk away from something just because it's hard. Even if you have to slow the tempo of a song or rhythm down to painfully slow speeds, you're still making progress and improving your technique. While you should challenge yourself, make sure you aren't trying to learn something that's too tough, too soon. Get down the basics before you try to master advanced rhythms and fast grooves.

Broken Sixteenth Note Fills

After your daily practice session, you should try putting together some of these beats and fills to make a song. Even if it's slow and basic, you'll still be learning important aspects of playing and song-writing. When you do this, focus on your transitions between rhythms, this is something a lot of drummers have trouble with. You should make the pieces fit together so that the overall rhythm flows together.

If you're practicing a lot or playing many fast tempos, you may find that your hands develop calluses from where the sticks come into contact with your palms and fingers. There are tapes available that you can put on your hands and fingers to protect them.

You should also make sure you're sticks aren't splintering your hands. As they wear out, they'll chip. Old pairs of sticks should be replaced to protect your hands and your drumheads.

Tips & Tricks

These expert tips and tricks come straight from professional drummers. Everything from setting up and practicing, to writing songs and performing live is covered on the following pages.

Practicing

1. As mentioned before, split up your practice time and your jam time. You should be practicing (technique, beats, rhythm) for at least 30 minutes every day (an hour is even better). After you practice, goof off, experiment, and play songs for another 45-60 minutes. Being able to apply everything you learn is extremely important.

2. Use a practice pad while you're doing mindless activities like watching television. It's a silent way to improve your grip and practice stick techniques. In addition to actual practice pads, you can also use a pillow. A pillow will obviously have no rebound, improving your strength and stamina.

3. Listen to the music you want to play. If you want to be a rock drummer, you need to listen to rock music. As you listen to new beats and rhythms, your brain will be subconsciously memorizing them. This also works for difficult songs. If there's a piece you're trying to learn, listen to it again and again. You need to know how something sounds before you can play it.

4. For similar reasons as number three, you should also listen to bands you may not typically choose. Many musicians tend to find certain beats, time signatures, or rhythms that they like and don't stray very far from what they've come to enjoy. If you only listen to the same few bands again and again, you want be hearing that many new rhythms. It's always recommended that you listen to new (and old) bands that you haven't heard before.

5. While you're looking for new bands to listen to, you should pick up other styles as well. Having some jazz, metal, and blues techniques will give you more variety when playing and make you a more versatile drummer.

6. **Drum Rudiments** (as you'll hear mentioned again and again) are made up of the singles, doubles, and other warm-ups we learned on page 14. These are the standard warm-up practices used by every drummer, no matter the level.

7. The three grips you should know are: Matched Grip (what we've been using), Traditional Grip, and French Grip. **Matched Grip** means you're holding both sticks the same way, with your palms facing down. **Traditional Grip** means you're holding your sticks with your palms facing up. **French Grip** means you're holding your sticks using only your fingers.

8. Just like we stated before, you should use a notebook to track your progress. Write down ideas you have, what you practiced that day, and how fast you could play.

9. You may consider learning a melodic instrument in addition to drums (like guitar or piano) to help you better understand harmony, song construction, and music theory.

10. "Overlearn" every song, fill, and beat; practice them again and again.

Layout & Setup

1. Be careful when **Cleaning Cymbals** as most products will remove logos. Some drummers swear that old cymbals, grime and all, have a warmer tone than clean ones.
2. Invest in a good seat. You'll be doing a lot of sitting, and you should make sure you're comfortable. Your seat should be adjustable in height and well padded.
3. **Ringing Cymbals** may be fixed by stuffing the hollow tubing of your stands with strips of cloth.
4. Check your snare wires regularly to make sure they're seated correctly. Also make sure to oil lugs and springs to keep your drum set working at its finest.
5. Cans of pressurized air can be used to clean the hard-to-reach areas of your drums, like corners, under hoops, and around lugs.

Performing &Recording

1. **Showmanship** is important to many drummers. You might find practicing in front of a mirror helpful in order to see how you can improve your posture and overall appearance.
2. Some drummers actually devote practice time to stick spinning, which is exactly what it sounds, while you're playing, toss one stick in the air and let it spin while you play the fill, then catch it and keep going. It's fun to learn and entertaining to watch.
3. Always keep a drum repair kit around, along with plenty of extra sticks when you gig.
4. Wear ear buds or noise cancelling headphones when you practice and gig. Drums are loud, especially the snare which was designed to carry across battlefields. Many drummers experience hearing loss after a few years of playing then start wearing **Ear Protection** after the fact. Be safe, not sorry.
5. Get stick holders that mount onto the stands of cymbals and keep many extra pairs around when you practice and perform.
6. You should always have a tuning key on you. Many drummers tie it to a string and keep it around their neck so they don't lose it.

Song –Writing

1. If you need inspiration, reverse your drum setup (i.e. if you normally play right-handed, switch to a left-handed setup) similar things have been done by musicians and artists for decades to inspire creativity (it'll also improve coordination and strengthen your weak hand).
2. To get you started, find a rhythm you really like then change it to fit your needs.
3. Riding the floor tom (instead of the hi-hat) will give your groove a deeper tone.
4. Adding more drums and cymbals to your set and experimenting with the new sounds may spark some inspiration.
5. Make sure to employ and practice **Volume Dynamics** (going from soft and quiet to deep and loud, and vice versa). It will affect your sound more than you think.

Moving On

Before you go, here are five things that you should never forget!

1. Practice everything you learn, over and over again. Even if you think you've got something down, keep practicing it. You can never be *too* good, even the professionals still study and practice regularly.

2. Keep an open mind and have respect for other musicians. We're all passionate about different things, remember that we all devote time to practice and have worked hard to get to where we are. Show good musicianship.

3. This is important if you want to be in a band: put yourself out there. You can't expect people to find you if you have no connections. In this day of technology, you're just making excuses if you say you can't post videos, make a website, or find other musicians.

4. As a drummer, you need to have versatility. Even if you only like rock music, you still need to be able to play all styles, because that's what good musicians do. As you progress, you should try forming the beats and rhythms you've learned into different styles. A sure sign of a good drummer is being able to take the same beat and mold it to fit any song and any style.

5. Have fun! Even if you're just sitting there trying to tune your drums by ear, enjoy it, there's no reason not to.

Now that you've finished book 1 in the Rock Drumming series, you can move on to book 2, which will teach you:

1. Triplets & Advanced Rhythm Counting
2. 100+ More Classic Beats
3. 50+ Essential Fills
4. Dozens more tips from the professionals

And more! You should never stop learning new things about your instrument, whether it is songs or technique; never stop trying to improve your playing.

In the meantime, you can find free resources, lessons, and more at LutxAcademy.com. If you need help, our friendly and free online community is filled with musicians of all levels, from beginner players to professional session artists. The guitarists, drummers, pianists, and bassists there will be happy to answer any of your music-related questions. Between the hundreds of members, there's always gear trades, jams, and friendly competitions going on, so feel free to join in at forum.lutzacademy.com!

Make sure to review, practice, and challenge yourself on a regular basis. Drumming should be fun and interesting, don't lose sight of that.

Now keep practicing!

Made in the USA
San Bernardino, CA
19 December 2014